JAMES DYER

# HILLFORTS OF ENGLAND AND WALES

SHIRE ARCHAEOLOGY

*Cover illustration*
Aerial view of Hambledon Hillfort (Dorset), looking south-west.
The hollows of huts and quarry scoops can be clearly seen
inside the ramparts.
(Photograph: J. E. Hancock)

Published by
SHIRE PUBLICATIONS LTD
Cromwell House, Church Street, Princes Risborough,
Aylesbury, Bucks, HP17 9AJ, UK.

Series Editor: James Dyer

ISBN 0 85263 536 2
First published 1981, reprinted 1985

Printed in Great Britain by
C. I. Thomas & Sons (Haverfordwest) Ltd,
Press Buildings, Merlins Bridge, Haverfordwest.

# Contents

# Acknowledgements

The author gratefully acknowledges the help he has received from Jeffrey May, who kindly read the work in manuscript and made numerous valuable suggestions. He is also indebted to Nicholas Thomas for allowing him to use unpublished material relating to Conderton Camp. Professor Richard Atkinson spent considerable time checking the figures given for the construction of Ravensburgh Castle, but I am responsible for any inaccuracies that may have crept into the calculations. Some of the line drawings are based partly on published sources, but with additions from the author's own observations. Unacknowledged photographs are by the author.

*In Memoriam*
S. E. Thomas
1924-1978

# List of illustrations

# 1
# Introduction

In 1962 the Ordnance Survey published its *Map of Southern Britain in the Iron Age,* which recorded some 1,366 hillforts or related earthworks (excluding the Isle of Man). In this book I have confined myself to the area of that map which covers the whole of England and Wales south of North Yorkshire and Cumbria and tends to form a coherent whole (fig. 1). A glance at the map shows concentrations of forts in south-west Wales, Cornwall and the Welsh Marches, with fairly thick distributions throughout the Cotswolds, Wessex and coastal North Wales. In the Peak District and Pennines the spread is fairly sparse, as it is in south-eastern England, whilst in Norfolk, Suffolk, the Fens and Lincolnshire very few examples exist at all. We will speculate on the reasons for this distribution later. Since the Ordnance Survey map was made other forts have been found by aerial photography and fieldwork.

Before we proceed further it is necessary to define our terms. The word *hillfort* suggests a defended structure on a hilltop, but many of the earthworks marked on the Ordnance Survey map would not fit this description since a large number are on lower or level ground. The word *fort* alone is not particularly helpful since it immediately suggests a military establishment, when, as we shall see, some sites were scarcely that. The earlier term *camp* is of no help and need not necessarily be of the correct historical period. The word *oppidum,* meaning literally a 'walled town', is reserved for urban settlements defended by complicated systems of linear dykes, introduced into south-east England in the first century BC by the Belgae. These are not hillforts as discussed in this book and are not considered here. In the event it seems best to retain the word *hillfort,* bearing in mind the above reservations.

What, then, is a hillfort? In the terms of this book it is a deliberately constructed fortification, built of earth, timber or stone, usually situated in an easily defended position, and frequently on a hilltop. It was constructed during the first millennium BC. Its purpose seems to have been essentially to offer the best protection possible to its inhabitants. Its size can vary from many examples under $\frac{1}{4}$ acre (0.1 ha) to some over 200 acres (80 ha). The majority lie between 3 and 30 acres (1.2 and 12 ha).

The defence usually consisted of one or more banks constructed from material either dug from a ditch in front of it or hewn from an internal quarry scoop. Material from cleaning the ditch was frequent-

ly thrown outwards and downhill to make an outer bank or counterscarp. In hillfort studies the word *bank* is used more or less syn-
onymously with *rampart*. In a small number of forts banks exist
without external ditches or quarry scoops, the rampart material having been scraped up from the surrounding area. Between the bank and
ditch there is often a flat platform or *berm*. In two thirds of the cases
in England and Wales the fort consists of only one banked and
ditched enclosure, termed *univallate*. Forts with additional lines of defence are termed *bivallate* (two), *trivallate* (three) and *multivallate*.
Nowadays the word *multivallate* is often applied to any fort with
more than one line of defence. Excavation often shows that multivallate forts are of more than one period of construction. Sites in
which the defences are set close together are described as *close-set* or
*compact*. Where they are widely spaced they are said to be *dispersed*.
Sometimes the defences are not concentric but tend to form wide
loops on one side or another; then these areas may be referred to as
*annexes*. In south-west Britain many forts can be seen with widely
spaced annexes ranged along the sides of hills. Sometimes additional
lines of defence only partially surround a fort. This is where the site
may have had a particular weakness to be overcome. In the stony
country of the west a number of forts are only defended by a stone
wall without a ditch (*walled-forts*). The material for construction was
either gathered from the surrounding land surface or from a slight
ditch or quarry scoop where it was almost impossible to dig in the
hard rocky ground. A final word may be said about forts that rely
almost entirely upon the natural steepness of ground for their defence:
these can occur anywhere that precipitous slopes are found and may
occasionally have been helped by man scarping a steep slope into a
vertical one. These might be better described as hilltop settlements.

It is possible to divide the forts into five main groups, determined
by the topography of the land on which they are built. These groups
are: 1, contour forts; 2, promontory forts; 3, plateau forts; 4, valley
forts; 5, multiple-enclosure or hillslope forts.

### 1. Contour forts (fig. 2)

To most observers these are the classic forts of the iron age.
Almost any reasonably upstanding hilltop may be crowned by a contour fort, in which one or more lines of defence run approximately
along the line of the same contour all the way round a hilltop, following the spurs and valleys as they occur. All the highest land inside the
defence thus becomes the fort. When seen in plan and divorced from
topographical features hillforts seem to be very curious shapes (fig. 2),
which has often given rise to the misapprehension that the builders

were incapable of constructing straight lines. Straight sides would have defeated the aim of contour fortification. The chosen hill does not have to be particularly high to carry a contour fort. Maiden Castle in Dorset is an excellent example of a low-eminence contour fort (80 feet or 25 metres above the surrounding land), whilst Hambledon Hill in the same county is a superb high-eminence example (328 feet or 100 metres above the clay land below).

## 2. Promontory forts (fig. 3)

Such forts rely on natural defence around most of their perimeter. The name speaks for itself. A promontory or spur is surrounded by steep scarp slopes, sea cliffs or a river gorge. Only on one or two sides is it joined to the main land mass, and at that point of weakness are man-made defences in the form of one or more lines of rampart and ditch, thus constructed to cut off the neck. This is a very economical sort of fort and was particularly popular, especially along the sea coasts, where the ocean surrounded three sides of what is often called a cliff-castle. Inland forts can be found on innumerable steep-sided spurs. As examples of both types we may quote The Rumps and Rame Head in Cornwall (cliff-castles) and Crickley Hill and Uleybury in Gloucestershire (promontory forts). The Dyke Hills in Oxfordshire lie at the confluence of the rivers Thames and Thame.

## 3. Plateau forts (fig. 4)

As their name implies plateau forts are sited on flat ground (often with land of a similar elevation all round). For their tactical strength they depended entirely on man-made defences and have no natural advantages of any kind, save perhaps access to a spring. Rainsborough Camp in Northamptonshire and Arbury Banks in Hertfordshire are good examples of this type of earthwork.

## 4. Valley forts

A rare subspecies related to the plateau forts is the valley fort, which is low-lying but makes up for its lack of tactical position by the considerable strength of its defence. Cherbury (Berkshire), Cassington Mill (Oxfordshire) and Risbury (Hereford and Worcester) are all examples.

## 5. Multiple-enclosure or hillslope forts (fig. 5)

These earthworks were built on the slope of a hill, completely overlooked from higher ground above. Clearly they are not in a strong military position and for an explanation we must look for a reason that required strength of construction, but not necessarily defence. It is usually suggested that they were stock enclosures of a specialised type, and it is noticeable that they are confined to south-western England and west Wales.

# 2
# The defences

When visiting hillforts today we see either grass-covered banks and U-shaped hollow ditches or perhaps the exposed tumbled walls of a stone-built fort. These may well be impressive: some ramparts still stand nearly 20 feet (6 m) above the interior and 38 feet (11 m) above the ditch bottom as at Bury Walls (Hereford and Worcester). In the majority of cases the bank is about 6 feet (2 m) above the interior, and the ditch is of similar depth. We can also expect to find a number of forts that are now reduced to heights in inches rather than feet, mainly owing to ploughing. Where stone walls exist, they may still rise to heights of 13 feet (4 m) and a width of 15 feet (4.5 m), as at Tre'r Ceiri in Gwynedd, but more often they survive only as a low scatter of overgrown boulders, perhaps 40 feet wide (12 m) as at Worlebury (Avon). Often forts have survived best in woodland, where man has been unable to reduce the earthworks by ploughing, and in remote areas where there has been no desire to remove the stone for more recent building purposes.

Ramparts are constructed of timber, stone or earth. To understand them we must turn to excavated examples. A chronological sequence has now emerged which seems to be fairly firmly based though future work may lead to minor modification. In most cases the simplest form of defence was a wooden palisade, either set directly into the ground or on top of a bank thrown up from an accompanying ditch. Such palisades have their origins in the bronze age at least and were constructed around farmsteads and villages to provide protection from wild animals and rustlers and to keep stock and children from wandering. A palisaded site like the farmstead of Staple Howe in North Yorkshire should probably be classed as a hillfort in embryo since its hump-backed hill has obviously been chosen for defence against human beings.

Many of the forts of the earliest iron age have revealed that they passed through a palisade stage, often long before a more substantial rampart was constructed. A simple stockade had surrounded the western half of Blewburton Hill (Oxfordshire) enclosing about half of the future 11 acre (4.4 ha) fort. At Dinorben (Clwyd) palisade slots were earlier than the *circa* fifth-century BC rampart. Numerous other sites show similar features. In the south of England it seems to have been the practice to embed the base of the palisade in earth, often the upcast from a ditch. Dates for these palisaded settlements are uncertain, but the seventh century BC does not seem unreasonable.

At about the same time, and much earlier in a few cases, box ramparts were constructed. These consisted of a double line of posts about 10 feet (3 m) apart. Horizontal timbers must have linked the back and front posts and also joined the uprights in each row together, thus providing a rigid frame. This is called lacing. Timbers were either tied, jointed or pegged together as no iron nails have been found. Soil from a ditch in front of the timbering was now placed inside the framework. Turves, stones or posts must have been attached at the front and rear to stop the soil from falling out. Perhaps planks were laid horizontally so that they could be built upwards as the amount of soil increased. Stuart Piggott's study of the unfinished fort of Ladle Hill in Hampshire (fig. 6) suggests that a more logical sequence of rampart building began with the cutting of a small marker ditch round the perimeter of the site. The turf, topsoil and chalk were then removed from the ditch and barrowed or carried in baskets about 75 feet (22 m) into the fort, where they were piled so as to leave the proposed line of the rampart clear. Larger blocks of chalk from deep down in the ditch were stacked in separate piles, probably for use in the core and facing of the rampart. The next stage, not reached at Ladle Hill, would have been to set up the timber framework for the box rampart. The large chalk blocks would then have been piled into it from behind, and the smaller chalk and topsoil placed on top, perhaps leaving the turf for a final retaining wall. Some kind of breastwork would have surmounted the whole structure. This method seems very logical, especially when building a fort on the edge of a steep hill: to throw the chalk upwards into a box rampart would have been almost impossible. Barry Cunliffe has called this earliest rampart stage the *Ivinghoe Beacon style*, after a hillfort in Buckinghamshire that seems to date between the eighth and seventh centuries BC (fig. 7). At Rams Hill in Berkshire Richard Bradley and Ann Ellison found the footings for a similar foundation, which, on radiocarbon evidence, could be as early as the twelfth century BC.

A classic series of hillfort excavations begun by the Curwens in 1925 revealed a further development, particularly at Hollingbury near Brighton (East Sussex), where their box rampart 8 feet wide (2.7 m) was found to be backed by a sloping wedge-shaped bank of similar width. This would have enabled the defenders to climb on to the rampart easily and would have given added strength to the whole structure. A similar rampart was excavated at South Cadbury (Somerset), where the whole rampart was $14\frac{1}{2}$ feet wide (4.4 m), the box structure being half of that width. Almost the same measurement occurred at Ravensburgh Castle (Hertfordshire), where the box rampart was $7\frac{1}{2}$ feet (2.3 m) wide and the sloping bank behind it 8 feet (2.4 m) wide.

The name *Hollingbury style* has long been given to this rampart type (fig. 7).

In North Wales the brilliant excavation of a small hillfort called Moel y Gaer, Rhosesmor (Clwyd), showed that the earliest rampart consisted of three parallel rows of posts. The outer row had upright posts at very close intervals of 2 to 3 feet (0.6-0.9 m). In between them was drystone walling. The rear row of posts was 20 feet (6 m) behind and seems to have acted principally as an anchor for the horizontal lacing timbers that linked the rows together. Between them was a more substantial central row of posts that were probably the main supports for the whole system and held the outer face firmly in position. In his excavation of Moel y Gaer rampart Graeme Guilbert found that it had been divided up into a number of box-like compartments, probably using hurdling, into which soil from different areas had been tipped. It has been suggested that this sort of construction would have been particularly useful when the timbering of the rampart was being repaired, provided it had not rotted away. However, this same type of cell-like construction has often been observed in earlier prehistoric sites, at the Giants' Hills long barrow in Lincolnshire and at Silbury Hill in Wiltshire, for example, and it may have some deep-seated origin in prehistoric engineering technique. Cunliffe has called this type of construction the *Moel y Gaer style*.

The Hod Hill defence is at present unique to that site (fig. 7). The front of the box rampart was embedded in a continuous palisade trench, whilst the rear row of posts rested on the ground surface and was not set into the subsoil at all. The front and back rows of posts were tied together with timber lacing, and the whole structure was filled with chalk rubble, whose weight held the woodwork rigidly in position.

It is not difficult to see the next progression. The rear row of posts disappears altogether, leaving only a front row of timbers with a massive wedge of soil piled behind them. On its own the palisade would be forced forwards by the weight of the soil and would collapse with such an arrangement, but it is probable that tying timbers ran back from those at the front into the body of the earth mound. This is known as the *Poundbury* (Dorset) *style* (fig. 7). It is found in a number of forts including Cissbury in West Sussex, and in excavations at Wandlebury in Cambridgeshire it was shown to be later than the Hollingbury style.

The greatest problem with all these rampart types is that they were not permanent. Wood rots (even if treated by charring), causing the face of the rampart to collapse. Perhaps as a result of this, somewhere about 350 BC the *glacis rampart* made an appearance (fig. 8). This was basically a dump of loose soil that continued the slope of the ditch side up to the rampart top, where there was probably a palisade and sometimes a retaining wall at the rear. A potential attacker had to scramble across the ditch and up a slope of loose, slipping scree in order to reach the top of the rampart. Some of these glacis slopes from ditch bottom to breastwork were of great height: Ravensburgh Castle (Hertfordshire) about 45 feet (14 m); Hod Hill (Dorset) 58 feet (17.4 m); and Maiden Castle (Dorset) 83 feet (25 m). In many cases the new glacis style replaced earlier ones. At Ravensburgh Castle, for example, a Hollingbury rampart had fallen into disrepair before the glacis style and V-shaped ditch were rapidly adopted as late as the first century BC. In many cases the glacis ramparts are much earlier, and one at Balksbury (Hampshire) possibly dates to the seventh or sixth century BC. At Maiden Castle (Dorset) the glacis rampart was modified at least six times and seems to have been regarded as the ultimate in rampart design.

Only in south-eastern England were there any further modifications. Here, with the approach of Roman forces from the mid first century BC onwards, the *Fécamp style* of defence was adopted, seemingly based on a northern Gaulish style of similar date (fig. 8). Basically it consisted of the cutting of a wide flat-bottomed ditch — 20 feet wide (6 m) at the Caburn in Sussex — and the piling of excavated material into a glacis bank, sometimes topped with a wooden palisade. Often this renewal buried earlier rampart types.

In those parts of England and Wales where good natural building stone occurs most forts were stone-built, although plenty of timber structures are also known. Sometimes there was a combination of stone and timber in which panels of drystone filled the gaps between vertical wooden posts arranged in the general style of a box rampart. Such work has been observed at Maiden Castle (Dorset) (Phase II) and South Cadbury; it is named after a German promontory fort as the *Preist style*. The rampart of a normal walled-fort consists of a neatly built front and rear facing of laid stone, with the interior of the wall filled with loose rubble. No foundation trench is dug, and the back of the wall is sometimes stepped and may have had a rampart walk. Rainsborough in Northamptonshire, dated to the sixth century BC, had a wall 17 feet wide (5.2 m) at the base, with two steps at the back (fig. 9). At Chalbury in Dorset Margaret Whitley uncovered a rubble-filled rampart 20 feet (6.1 m) thick with drystone facing at the front and rear. This hillfort can be dated to somewhere around 450 BC on pottery evidence. As was usual, material for both these forts was quarried from an irregular ditch on their outer sides. One of the most impressive stone-walled forts is Tre'r Ceiri in Gwynedd (fig. 9).

The stone for its construction was gathered from the hillside and quarried from rocky outcrops, and there was no formal ditch. The fort wall still stands 13 feet high (4 m) and has parts of its rampart walk, and access steps for the sentries, still intact. It was still in use during the late Roman period. A number of stone-walled forts were later rebuilt with glacis ramparts: Rainsborough (Northamptonshire) and Llanmelin (Gwent) are famous examples.

In the north-west of our region, from Wales to Yorkshire, spreading as far south-west as the Cotswolds, *timber-laced forts* have been observed. They seem to have developed in Scotland as early as the seventh century but may also have developed independently in the Cotswold region. Such forts involve the combination of layers of drystone walling with rows of horizontal timbers placed either longitudinally or transversely through the core, presumably to give the structure greater strength and stability. Maiden Castle in Cheshire and Castle Ditch in the same county both passed through this stage. Philip Dixon found signs of horizontal timbers passing from back to front through the stone rampart at Crickley Hill (period 2). The ends of the timbers were exposed in the wall faces at back and front, a length of 19 feet (5.8 m). Forts in which the timbers lie both longitudinally and transversely and are fixed with nails are known on the European continent as *murus gallicus* but have not yet been found in Britain.

In Scotland at least sixty timber-laced forts show signs of vitrification. In these cases the timbers have caught fire and the great heat has caused the stones to fuse together. Whether the firing was accidental or deliberate is a matter for debate, but in all probability it was the result of attack or accident. Southern British forts showing signs of vitrification are rare, but Wincobank at Sheffield is certain and both Caer Euni and Pendinas in Clwyd seem to be possible examples.

Evidence for sentry walks on top of the different types of rampart is rare, but their existence is assumed. Only in a few Welsh sites do examples still survive. In the earthen forts a wooden breastwork almost certainly crowned the defences.

Late in the history of many hillforts the idea of multivallation was introduced: the building of a second rampart and ditch, usually outside the first, to increase the defence of the fort in depth. Multivallation was almost certainly introduced to counter sling warfare. A slinger on top of a high rampart could sling with accuracy about 120 yards (110 m) downhill, whilst an attacker slinging uphill had his range severely curtailed. At Maiden Castle (Dorset) the ramparts were sufficiently widely spaced to make slinging out highly effective but to minimise the dangers from slinging inwards.

With the exception of those in the Fécamp style, hillfort ditches are usually V-shaped. How much this is due to subsequent erosion of near-vertical sides is uncertain. Considering that they were probably dug with antler picks and spades made from wood, the achievement is considerable and we may ponder on the effort required. Calculations have been made at Ravensburgh Castle (Hertfordshire) (fig. 8) for the work involved in digging the ditch surrounding the 22 acre fort (8.9 ha) using figures for the length of the ditch as 3,982 feet (1,214 m) and its cross-section as 138 square feet (12.8 sq m). This results in a volume of 549,516 cubic feet (15,562 cu m) of chalk removed. Assuming that this was then carried upwards and placed inside the box rampart to form a bank with rampart walk 9 feet high (2.7 m), then the work is likely to have taken about 170,000 man hours. (This calculation is based on the work studies carried out during the construction of the experimental earthwork on Overton Down in 1960.)

The amount of wood required in constructing the rampart is quite staggering, particularly when we realise that the straight rows of trees found in modern plantations were not available. Instead oak is most likely to have been used, and efforts may have been made to coppice it. The total perimeter length of the main rampart at Ravensburgh Castle was 1,300 yards (1,190 m). Excluding extra timber for gateways, the box rampart alone would have required 1,190 main posts at the back and front of the structure, spaced at $6\frac{1}{2}$ foot (2 m) intervals (each being about 15 feet or 4.5 m long and 8 inches or 200 mm in diameter), and a further 5,950 lacing posts, each $8\frac{1}{4}$ feet (2.5 m) long and at least 4 inches (100 mm) in diameter, whilst the rampart face would be clad with 11,900 poles 13 feet (4 m) long and 4 inches (100 mm) in diameter. This provides a minimum of 19,040 lengths of timber. Modern estimates suggest that using a light iron-age axe, and frequently resharpening it, a man might fell and trim the lop and top from one oak tree 8 inches (200 mm) in diameter and 50 feet (15 m) high over all in about an hour and three-quarters with at least fifteen minutes spent stacking the trimmings. It would take him about another forty minutes to cut the trunk into three lengths of 15 feet (4.5 m) each and clear the ground for the next felling. This means a time of about fifty minutes per post, with a production rate of about ten posts of this size in a working day of eight hours. The 4 inch (100 mm) diameter posts would require about twenty minutes per post or twenty-four posts per eight-hour day. The larger timbers would thus take up 992 man hours work, whilst the 4 inch (100 mm) diameter posts would take two-thirds of the time, about 661 man hours work. The timber would have been cut some distance from the fort and had to be transported on carts which required two men to load. This involved about 160 cart loads, which with time for loading and unloading probably took a further 213 man hours (one hour twenty minutes per load). Larger timbers may have been dragged by oxen.

### Ravensburgh Castle hillfort: construction time

circumference 1,190 m

*Timber*

| | |
|---|---:|
| Large posts (front and rear) | 1190 required |
| Lacing posts | 5950 required |
| Cladding posts | 11900 required |
| *Total separate timbers* | 19040 required |
| | |
| Cutting time – large posts | 992 man hours |
| Cutting time – small posts | 661 man hours |
| Transport time (2 men) | 416 man hours |
| Digging post holes | 595 man hours |
| Erecting large posts (45 minutes) | 893 man hours |
| Lacing posts (tying 5 minutes) | 498 man hours |
| Cladding posts (tying 5 minutes) | 992 man hours |
| *Total time* | 5047 man hours |

*Ditches and rampart* (assuming bare hillside)

| | |
|---|---:|
| Digging ditch and filling box rampart | 170,000 man hours |
| *Total* | 175,047 man hours |

Allowing an eight-hour day:

| | | |
|---|---:|---:|
| | 1 man | 21,880 days |
| | 10 men | 2,188 days |
| | 100 men | 219 days |
| | 200 men | 109 days |

Of course, such figures are very rough estimates. We do not know how much help was given by women and children. The weather and the length of daylight will have played a vital role, as will the daily life of the community. With animals to tend and farm crops to be harvested, it is unlikely that work was continuous, unless the inhabitants were working under stress conditions, with attack imminent. In such a case, a medium-sized fort like Ravensburgh might have been constructed in about four months.

# 3
# Entrances

The point of greatest weakness in any fort was its gate, and even in the largest earthworks the number of entrances was kept to a minimum. A large fort like Stanwick (North Yorkshire), with an area of nearly 850 acres (340 ha), had only three gates in its 4 miles (6.4 km) of outer earthwork. Entrances were particularly vulnerable to attack from battering and fire, and elaborate attempts were often made to make if difficult for attackers to reach the actual gates, by throwing up external earthworks or creating blind passages.

The simplest entrance consisted of a gap in the rampart and a corresponding causeway across any accompanying ditch. Sometimes no physical gate was present and we are reminded of Caesar's reference to Bigbury (Kent) where all the entrances were blocked by felled trees laid close together. More probably a simple blocking of planks on trestles or thorn bushes dragged into place may have served to keep cattle from straying: only an emergency would have required something stronger. Light fences or walls may have been set up round the ends of the ditches to prevent anyone from falling into them. Entrances without gates have been excavated at Conderton Camp (Hereford and Worcester) and at Ravensburgh Castle (Hertfordshire), south-east entrance.

Usually there is a passage between the rampart ends lined with timber or stone or both (figs. 11, 19). This may be blocked by one or more gates. Sometimes the width of the passage made it necessary for a double gate with a blocking stone or posthole at the centre. It seems very likely, from the arrangement of postholes found, that most entrances were crossed by a timber bridge that carried a rampart walk from one side to the other. Suggestions for watch-towers constructed over the gate are interesting but have been dismissed, since they would be very vulnerable to destruction by fire. However, they seem to have worked in the American West.

Deep postholes in the entrance passage show where the gateposts stood, and one suspects the presence of a linking lintel between them. How the gates were hung presents a problem. No hinges have been found, and except for a possible iron pivot ring at Hembury (Devon) and a pivot from South Cadbury (Somerset) we can only speculate as to their suspension. Michael Avery is probably correct when he suggests a pintle and socket, 'where one side member of a wooden door frame projects above and below the door panelling and pivots in socket holes at top and bottom'. Claims have also been made for the door being hinged at the top to open up and outwards, or to be raised like a portcullis, but there is no evidence to support either. A slot across the entrance at Croft Ambrey (Hereford and Worcester) might even be considered as the first cattle grid!

The width of the entrance passage would determine whether the gate had one or two leaves to it. Recesses on either side of some passages indicate that two doors were meant to fold back into them when open, and when closed they would rest against a blocking stone, whose base was firmly buried beneath the road surface.

Hillfort entrances may have been designed with a certain amount of vanity and local pride. The desire to impress is a very strong human impulse, and an elaborate defence may have been one way of demonstrating social status and wealth by the grandeur of architectural design, as well as increasing the builders' sense of security.

Where a fort had two or more ramparts it was often the custom to stagger the entrances (fig. 10b), so that the person entering had to turn to the left for some distance, thus exposing his unshielded sword side to defenders on the rampart above. This can be well observed at Chun Castle in Cornwall. Sometimes the terrain made it necessary to turn the entrance to the right as at Hod Hill (Dorset), in which case the defenders may have manned the outer right-hand rampart. Any method that extended the time taken to enter the fort seems to have been tried, in order to keep the entrant under observation for as long as possible. Consequently it became the custom to experiment with defence in depth and long extensions were added to the passages leading into the fort. These are sometimes called inturned entrances, or Bredon entrances (after Bredon Hill, Hereford and Worcester) (fig. 10a). They are particularly common on the Welsh borders and in the Cotswolds. Less often the entrance passage might be turned outwards forming a forward passage, sometimes with bastions as at Battlesbury (Wiltshire). In a number of excavated examples it is clear that the inturn was a later thought added on to a simple entrance. There would be gates at either end of the passage and one assumes that attackers would be trapped between the two gates until they had been scrutinised and disarmed. Also within the inturned passageway it was sometimes the custom to provide some kind of guard chamber for the keeper of the gate (fig. 11). Some of these are very tiny, little more than sentry boxes (Maiden Castle, Dorset), and could not have been lived in permanently. Others are extensive guard chambers with evidence of hearths and space for beds, like Burrough Hill (Leicestershire) measuring 28 feet (8.5 m) by 18 feet (5.5 m) (fig. 17). These were all designed as an integral part of the entrance passage and were often paired. Sometimes guard chambers seem to have been an afterthought and were simply huts placed closest to the gate as at Moel y Gaer, Rhosesmor (Clwyd) and Conderton Camp (Hereford and Worcester) (fig. 18).

The roadway running through the entrance tended to become very worn and might have to be renewed with local cobblestones as many as twenty times. Frequently wheeled traffic wore grooves into the road surface, which careful excavation has revealed. Where possible in stone country the road surface would be the exposed natural rock, which could stand a lot of wear, but in the chalk lands erosion was rapid and surfaces of puddled chalk (chalk into which small flints were deliberately pounded) were sometimes used; this retarded the erosion but eventually led to the formation of hollow ways up to the fort entrance.

Two postholes inside the entrance at Rainsborough (Northamptonshire) and two more at St Catherine's Hill (Hampshire) have been interpreted as footings for triumphal arches or totem poles connected with some tribal ritual. At Maiden Bower (Bedfordshire) a pit in the centre of the entrance passage contained the mixed-up and partially burnt bones of about fifty people as well as animals and birds. Above this was a small chalk cist containing three human bones: a sort of token burial over the others below (fig. 12).

The more elaborate entrances incorporate the construction of outworks in front of the gateways. At Crickley Hill (Gloucestershire) a bank curves outwards from the main rampart to form a hornwork reminiscent of a medieval barbican, with a gate at the outer end of it. From the top of the hornwork the defenders had complete control over everyone entering. At the entrance to Blackbury Castle, Devon, the ramparts turned outwards and a triangular annexe was added with a barbican-like entrance passage about 150 feet (45 m) long leading to the main gate, and also closed by a gate at its outer end. The second phase of Maiden Castle (Dorset) also had a similar triangular annexe, but this led to double gateways. Again it could be controlled by men on the rampart above. Barry Cunliffe's excavation of the eastern entrance at Danebury gives a good idea of the care that sometimes went into designing the 'perfect' entrance (fig. 10c). The main entrance passage ran outwards from the fort with an extension stretching about 160 feet (50 m) on its right-hand side. Here a high flint and timber-faced hornwork formed what Barry Cunliffe called a command post. It stood at the centre of the entrance complex and from it it was possible to supervise two gates, the outer hornworks and much of the fort ditches, all within a distance of 180 to 200 feet (60-70 m), an easy range for a competent slinger. Perhaps the most magnificent of all outworks are those at the two entrances to Maiden Castle (Dorset). Both have a maze of ramparts and ditches, which make a direct approach impossible, and Mortimer Wheeler's pioneering excavation of the simpler of the two has given a most plausible explanation of its use. Slingers' platforms, some with thousands of slingstones still in position, were uncovered. Numerous blind alleys had been provided in an attempt to fool the attackers. Study of the plans of this fort are well worthwhile.

In the choosing of isolated hilltops for forts it sometimes happened that only one possible entrance position could be found and this was not always in the most appropriate place. On such occasions special efforts would be made to protect it. These might include the construction of a *chevaux-de-frise*. This consisted of small blocks of preferably pointed stones set on end in the ground at close intervals over an area outside the gate or any point of weakness. Such an arrangement would slow down any mass attack and would certainly break the legs of horses which charged through them. Pointed stakes may also have been used for the same purpose, but these have not survived or been detected, since few people excavate outside hillforts. *Chevaux-de-frise* are rare in England and Wales but can be seen at Pen-y-Gaer (Clwyd), still standing 1 foot tall (0.3 m), and at Craig Gwrtheyrn in Dyfed. At Carn Alw, also in Dyfed, the ground is thickly strewn with apparently natural boulders, which serve a similar function. Walking across a *chevaux-de-frise* makes a noisy clatter, making it almost impossible to approach the fort unheard. A restricted site also led to difficult approaches to the fort, sometimes following rather narrow ledges along precipitous hillsides. This had the advantage of making a massed attack impossible and usually meant that the approach could be closely watched from above, as at Caer Caradoc (Church Stretton, Shropshire) or the south-eastern entrance of Hambledon Hill (Dorset).

# 4
# Interiors

Since about 1960 excavations have concentrated on examining hillfort interiors and this is giving us a clearer picture of how they were arranged. It is becoming evident that whilst some forts seem to have had a random distribution of houses, others have been carefully planned with streets regularly laid out and lined with buildings. In other cases settlement was concentrated in specific areas of the fort whilst other parts were left empty, perhaps for livestock.

Examination of building types shows that the earliest structures in many excavated forts were four-post features which have been interpreted as granaries (fig. 13). Indeed, at Crickley Hill (Gloucestershire) two of them had been full of barley when they were burnt down. This type of building tends to be between 9 and 12 feet square (2.7 and 3.6 m), and alternative interpretations of its function have been offered. At Grimthorpe (Yorkshire) it has been suggested that the buildings were of two storeys with granaries below and watch-towers above. However, at Croft Ambrey (Hereford and Worcester) hundreds of regularly placed four-post huts seem to have occupied the site, so watch-towers would be an unlikely explanation for most of those, and an enormous capacity for grain storage would be implied if they were granaries. Many of the Croft Ambrey buildings were rebuilt on the same spot a number of times, so this indicates a long period of occupation for the fort. At Crickley Hill (Gloucestershire) Philip Dixon has excavated a series of longhouses or aisled halls bearing similarities to rectangular houses of the same period in western Europe. Some people would interpret these as rows of four posters, but four-post buildings are very wasteful of resources, which can be better employed if a number are joined together in rows. An alternative to the granary interpretation is as a series of barracks, and this must be given careful thought when we come to consider the regional purpose of forts.

Four-post structures seem to have been in use in Britain between the ninth and fifth centuries BC. During this period circular houses came into use, in most cases following the rectangular buildings. At Moel y Gaer, Rhosesmor (Clwyd), round houses with stake-walls were constructed with large posts to support the porches. Exactly how they were roofed is something of a mystery (fig. 13). More substantial houses were constructed elsewhere with walls indicated by rings of posts or footing trenches, and traces of wattle and daub.

Thatch or turf would have provided a roof for a building perhaps 15 feet (4.5 m) high. Such houses might average 24 feet (7.3 m) in diameter, with a ring of posts supporting the roof about 6 feet (1.8 m) inside the walls. This would leave a clear central area about 12 feet across (3.6 m), which would give ample room for a hearth and movement area. Around the walls a number of compartments might be screened off as sleeping areas, and the high roof would allow for galleries where children might sleep and goods be stored. Such huts would be dark and filled with smoke, although the four central posts at Little Woodbury (Wiltshire) suggest that some kind of louvre might have existed. There seem to have been almost as many variations to the design of round houses as there are of modern houses, so we need not look too closely for comparisons.

Possibly the most intriguing iron-age building in Britain was a rectilinear structure about 180 feet square (55 sq m) excavated recently at Pilsdon Pen in Dorset. The building, on wooden sleeper beams, enclosed an approximately square courtyard that had originally been occupied by circular huts. Unfortunately insufficient survived to make a credible reconstruction of the building, but its size suggests something on a grand scale.

In stone country house walls were of drystone, some standing about 4 feet (1.2 m) high. The foundations of many of these can still be seen in Wales today, at Tre'r Ceiri, or in and around Carn Fadrun, both in Gwynedd. Often a stone porch was added to ensure that the prevailing wind did not whistle through the house.

In England unexcavated hillforts often show surface evidence of houses, their circular hollows still being visible on the ground at sites like Hod Hill (Dorset) or Beacon Hill (Hampshire). On steeper land hut platforms can be identified as semicircular terraces cut into the hillside. Where the fort has been ploughed house circles may well appear on aerial photographs, as with the dense occupation of the Dyke Hills (Oxfordshire), or Arbury Banks (Hertfordshire), where a single house is visible.

Excavation has failed to differentiate between the function of individual round houses with any accuracy. We cannot talk of streets of shops or inns for example. Particular contents may indicate that the owner wove cloth, prepared skins, worked bronze or iron or shaped wood and perhaps made pottery, but we do not know if the products were sold from the house or taken to a market area within the town or even hawked around the neighbouring countryside.

Perhaps the most common features of the fort interior are grain-storage pits dug into the solid chalk or limestone, or lined with drystone or wickerwork in softer soils. Early storage pits seem to have been quite small, but by the third and second centuries BC they were about 6 feet (1.8 m) deep, with slightly narrower diameters, and held about 44 bushels of corn. These pits seem to have been used for grain storage for a few years before they became sour and were used as rubbish dumps. Basketry or clay linings helped to keep the grain dry, and sometimes fires were lit in the pits before filling to kill algae and bacteria and to dry the walls. The pits were sealed with clay or dung and, provided they were kept airtight, grain could be kept for several months, eventually to be used for seed corn or flour. In forts that were occupied for long periods it was inevitable that filled-in pits would be cut into by new pits from time to time. Then drystone work was needed to prevent the sides from falling in, as at Conderton Camp (Hereford and Worcester) (fig. 20). In the mountainous country of north and west Wales storage pits do not occur, and this can be explained both by the difficulty of digging solid rock and by the economy of the forts, which was based on livestock, instead of arable farming. Some pits were used as latrines once their grain storage function had ceased. Associated postholes may indicate covering sheds. The archaeology of latrines is a subject that has not been studied closely!

Although not strictly a function of the fort's interior, mention must be made of water supply. Very few forts have springs rising inside them, though Ambresbury Banks and Loughton Camp in Epping Forest are examples that do. In most cases springs rise on the lower slopes of the hill outside the fort, sometimes as much as half a mile (800 m) away. Study shows that very few forts are more than a mile from a water supply (fig. 14). One envisages trails of women carrying water vessels backwards and forwards to their houses. Even with a higher prehistoric water table, the distance would have been notable. This suggests that attacks on forts expected to be short and sharp, with no prolonged siege in which lack of water supply would have resulted in the fort's downfall. Only the Romans are known to have resorted to such tactics. Special gateways were built close to the water supply for easy access, as at Hod Hill (Dorset). Alternative water supplies have been suggested, such as natural ponds and dew ponds or water from the eaves drip of hut roofs channelled into clay-lined storage pits. The former have not been found in excavations, and there is limited evidence for the latter. Gullies connected with huts certainly seem to be related to drainage, but specific attempts to retain the water are difficult to substantiate.

Forts may have been the spiritual centres of the iron age. Many people have drawn attention to the possibility of their providing a religious focus for the community. There was an apparent tradition of building forts on sites already occupied by semi-religious monuments like long barrows (Bratton Camp, Wiltshire), causewayed camps (The Trundle, West Sussex) or bronze-age barrow cemeteries (Old Winchester Hill, Hampshire). Three forts have produced the footings of buildings that may have been temples. At South Cadbury (Somerset) what was almost certainly a shrine stood near the centre of the fort. It was square, with a porch, and had been built about AD 43. A processional way led to the temple, and on either side of it deposits of animal bones, including an ox, and weapons had been buried. At Danebury (Hampshire) a group of rectangular buildings facing towards the eastern gate, and close to the road, are considered to have had a religious function. In the older excavation at Maiden Castle (Dorset) of 1934-7, it was noticed that the main road from the eastern gate ran directly to a circular stone building 30 feet (9 m) in diameter. This structure was later replaced by a smaller circular Roman building that stood beside a square Romano-Celtic temple. As the excavator, Mortimer Wheeler, observed, 'the almost ostentatious barbarism of the little building standing in the shadow of the four-square temple . . . justifies perhaps the passing fantasy that here we may have a tangible witness to that continuity of cult which has often been suggested in regard to Romano-Celtic temples.' Before we are finally convinced by these arguments, we might just consider these structures in more secular roles: town halls perhaps, though scarcely big enough for the civic banquets hinted at in Irish Celtic literature.

Excavations of forts have often produced human burials, perhaps lying in the ditches, buried in storage pits or scattered and mutilated outside the fort entrance. These cases can be seen either as victims of war or perhaps dedicatory burials. Serious attention has not been given to planned hillfort cemeteries, since we would expect these to lie outside the fort, where excavation is unlikely to have taken place. At Maiden Castle Mortimer Wheeler found the war cemetery outside the eastern gateway but within the hornworks, on the spot where the traditional cemetery already existed. Future work on forts should also consider locating the graveyards.

An unusual aspect of Celtic religion was the digging of shafts, often many feet deep, that seem to have acted as entrances to the underworld. Into these, sacrifices, both of people and animals, were dispatched at regular intervals. Sometimes wrongly identified as wells, probable examples exist at Painswick Beacon (Gloucestershire) and Cadbury Castle (Devon) 58 feet deep (17.6 m). At Danebury examples dating from neolithic times have been found, again stressing the possible continuous sanctity of the hill over thousands of years.

# 5
# Function and situation

We have hinted that some hillforts grew out of religious centres, as did many medieval towns. Similarly other hillforts must have grown as market centres or military installations. Many were traditional meeting places, on hilltops, where farming communities of the late bronze age had come together to air their differences. A barrow might mark the spot, or boundary ditches marking the edges of their territory might all meet on the summit, as they do at Quarley Hill (Hampshire). At such places a few houses were perhaps built with an essentially farming background, but as time went by the farming gave way to trading. Some animals were still kept, but commerce began to interest the residents. The provision of a palisade for protection against wild animals is easily accepted, and so the defended hilltop site begins its slow progression to the great hillfort of later years. Such forts might be peripheral to a region. Others grew at its centre, because this was more convenient for people of the same tribal background. These central places probably developed from small villages, each with certain advantages, but one with more in its favour than the others – perhaps it was easier to reach as trackways met there, it was near the bridging point of a river or marsh or its products were better liked than its neighbours', or maybe it was close to a religious sanctuary which attracted pilgrims. At all events it flourished whilst others were bypassed. In spite of this its inhabitants do not seem to have been more important than those outside. They used the same pottery vessels and metal tools. Unfortunately we do not find golden torcs and ceremonial shields that might make us think otherwise. In most cases we are simply seeing a different role being played: a trading centre as opposed to a farming community.

There is no doubt that a lot of villages were permanently occupied for relatively long periods of time, and it is these that we can use to draw parallels to medieval walled towns, the market or religious centres mentioned above. However, some forts that have been excavated show signs of having been used as storage centres: the rows of four-post structures found at Croft Ambrey or Danebury suggest that here perhaps was a fortified store where surplus supplies of food or other goods could be centralised, and from where they could be distributed to areas in need. This implies a strictly controlled society in which everyone played an essential part. Crop producers brought their surplus to the fort for redistribution. Or was the crop a form of tax extracted from the farmer as tribute to a king or chieftain? This certainly suggests a warrior overlord. Is that why the distribution centre was fortified with massive earthworks and gates renewed many times? It seems a little unnecessary otherwise. The idea is hard to accept and yet the sort of society it suggests might be sufficiently motivated to build great earthworks for the public good or because they were forced to do so. Perhaps we should be looking for the magnificent graves of such powerful princes. Clearly this sort of fort was very different from the walled town.

It was also different from those forts which were military centres, for, surely, some of the earthworks must have contained barracks in which warriors were based? Sadly, there is no proof. On surface evidence alone it is not possible to recognise such sites, but we might find clues by considering medieval parallels. Military installations tended to be spread along the borders between one country and another. Is it possible that concentrations of forts in England and Wales could indicate boundary zones between alien Celtic societies. The densest concentrations are to be found along the Welsh Marches and the Cotswolds, and less distinctly in southern England. Suppose the Marcher forts represent a warring zone between what we might call the proto-Welsh tribes and the proto-Midlanders — a situation later reflected in the building of Offa's Dyke and the Principality of Wales. Such an organisation of forts suggests a centralised government trying to control a society that remained turbulent for a millennium. Of course, the forts are not all contemporary, and some will be early and replaced by others more suited to specific local conditions.

In south-west England were the multiple-enclosure or hillslope forts, whose overlooked position on the hillside, with a series of wide enclosures or annexes surrounding a central circular or oval one, could well have provided protection for large herds of cattle, many of which might be gathered together for export to the continent from Cornish and Devon ports. Multiple-enclosure forts seem to date to the second and first centuries BC. Good examples include Clovelly Dykes and Milber Down, both in Devon (fig. 5). Whilst in the south-west a group of banked and ditched enclosures known as rounds should not be overlooked. Seldom more than 2 acres (0.8 ha) in area, they seem to have been defended farmsteads of iron-age date, many of which continued to function in the Roman period. Their distribution in Cornwall is very dense and they may well have been low in the social order which had multiple-enclosure forts at its middle and stone-walled forts like Chun Castle (only 170 feet across, 52 m) and Castle-an-Dinas (6 acres, 2.4 ha) at its head. These Cornish sites do not compare with the great hillforts of Wessex and we should probably see them simply as the strongholds of a local nobility.

When we turn to Wessex and southern England we find a wide distribution of large contour forts, with few small examples, spaced out mostly into territories of between 40 and 50 square miles (65 to 80 sq km). This is a reasonable size if the forts can be seen as distribution or collection centres, though those on the south coast may have developed cross-channel trade, perhaps through Hengistbury Head (Dorset). Excavation indicates that occupation was often sporadic and infrequent, and the area may be seen as relatively peaceful, thus giving trade a chance to develop. Where small forts did exist they seem to have gone out of use before the third century BC, leaving only the developed hillfort to command its territory. These territories seem to have an approximately equal proportion of chalk upland and riverside watermeadows (fig. 14). This means that although the fort was fully developed, it still depended on agriculture and livestock for its subsistence, and aerial survey shows fields outside many earthworks that would have been used for grain production (fig. 15). In some cases the territory of the fort is clearly defined from its neighbour by a river or dyke. In others the demarcation line has disappeared and can only be guessed at. In the Chilterns a series of cross-ridge dykes and stockades separated one territory from another, such as Dray's Ditches (Bedfordshire) (fig. 16).

Some areas of England lack forts in any number. These are east Kent, east Yorkshire and East Anglia and Lincolnshire. East of Wandlebury near Cambridge in East Anglia there are only half a dozen sites with the exception of the multivallate plateau fort at Warham (Norfolk) and the nearby possible beachhead fort of Holkham. What does this great blank on the fort map mean? There are plenty of low hills available, but the Ordnance Survey map shows few iron-age sites of any kind. Aerial photography and excavation show that the region was occupied throughout the iron age, with farmsteads and open villages, some very large and rich like Dragonby in Lincolnshire. The social system was obviously organised in a way that did not require the construction of many forts. Law and order were controlled in some way which discouraged casual raids and cattle rustling by neighbouring villages and yet was strong enough to rally everyone to the flag when danger threatened at the approach of Caesar or the Boudican revolt. Perhaps this involved mobile warfare using chariots as the main armament. This would make sense when considered in conjunction with the various dykes that have been found in eastern England, and the cross-ridge dykes of the southern downs, which would have been great obstacles to chariot movements.

# 6
# When, who and why?

I have left till last those questions which it is most difficult to answer. We have already gone some way to seeing when hillforts were built. As early as the neolithic period about 3500 BC a few hilltops were being fortified in a manner that might constitute the beginnings of hillforts. Carn Brea (Cornwall) and Crickley Hill (Gloucestershire) are examples. It was early in the first millennium BC that numerous palisaded hilltop settlements were appearing all over southern Britain, though the majority of true forts with earthen ramparts and ditches developed between 750 and 500 BC. Over the next two hundred years some forts were strengthened and new and stronger examples developed, often with indications of careful planning of internal features. During the third and second centuries BC a number of large forts emerged as territorial capitals, and many smaller ones were abandoned. In south-eastern Britain many forts seem to have been hastily refortified at the time of Caesar. During the same period some of the population moved to valley sites, to the so-called *oppida,* some of which were defined by massive linear earthworks. There has been much debate on the meaning of the word *oppida*. Generally speaking, they were literally 'walled towns' and formed tribal capitals for wide areas, perhaps with a complicated layout of streets and industrial areas, and a mint for coin production. They enclosed much larger areas than the hillforts, and examples have been identified at Camulodunum (Colchester), Prae Wood (St Albans), Silchester and Bagendon (Gloucestershire). An oppidum has been defined as a 'defended town with an economy largely dependent on semi-industrialised manufacturing and trade'. By their very nature and siting, they are not hillforts and so lie outside the scope of this book.

In many cases hillforts remained in use until the Roman occupation, and those in the south-west were called upon to defend themselves against the attacks of Vespasian around AD 45. Maiden Castle and Hod Hill were amongst twenty towns that he 'subdued'. Many hillforts were slighted and made unfit for occupation, and the tribespeople were moved from them to new towns on lower ground, such as Dorchester (from Maiden Castle and Poundbury) or Wroxeter (from the Wrekin, Shropshire). In the highland areas forts remained occupied for much of the Roman period. By the third century AD some of the English forts seem to have had partial reuse, with a temple at Maiden Castle for instance, and by the fourth century there was occupation at Norbury and Ring Hill (both Gloucestershire) and the great temple complex dedicated to the god Nodens at Lydney (Gloucestershire). In Wales it is suggested that some forts were reoccupied against Irish raiders, but this is questionable, and a reuse for religious purposes seems more likely. During the next three centuries a number of hillforts were refortified and occupied in one way or another. South Cadbury (Somerset), Castle Dore and Chun Castle (Cornwall) and Dinas Emrys (Gwynedd) are but four examples. Leslie Alcock has pointed out that some forts which on surface evidence appear to be typically iron-age in design may have been built entirely in the post-Roman period. The same may be true of sites in eastern England that could be of Viking construction. Clare Camp (Suffolk) is a possible example.

But there is another aspect of the question 'When were hillforts built?' Earlier I gave some figures for the possible length of time taken to build Ravensburgh Castle (Hertfordshire). I suggested that under stress the fort might have been built by two hundred men in four months, with aid from women and children, as well as a period of favourable weather. But most fort building took place between 750 and 500 BC. Was that a period of continuous stress? If so, what caused it? There are hints that at this time immigrants arrived bringing with them new pottery styles and ironworking, rectangular huts and the Celtic language. The first two of these have been detected at South Cadbury (Somerset). If this is a valid argument, and many archaeologists are reluctant to accept it, then we can see these earliest forts being constructed as a response to invasion: some by the invaders and some by the invaded. However, in a time of stress the population might have little time for fort construction. Many continental forts seem to have been built during periods of relative stability. Clearly the best time for fort building was during a time of peace, when the builders could concentrate on the best way to design a particular feature, and when the work could be fitted into the daily routine of farming life. Under such circumstances two years might seem a more likely period of construction, with the possibility of modifications in design as the work progressed.

If we do not accept the theory of immigration between 750 and 500 BC then we must seek an answer on a smaller scale in the gradual expansion of farming territories and efforts to prevent land stealing and cattle rustling. The chalk downlands are covered with Celtic fields arranged around hillforts and open villages, with linear dykes dividing one group from another and clearly defining territorial limits often of 30 to 40 square miles (80-100 sq km). In the south-west the moorland was divided in a similar way by boundary banks called reaves. Settled

life within these territories led to an increase in population, and
larger population meant that greater social control was necessary to
avoid conflict with one's neighbours. Social control implies the choosing of leaders and a scale of hierarchy, which goes largely undetected
in archaeology. This hierarchy might be reflected in the size of particular hillforts, but again this is difficult to identify. Nor should we
see the same system of social control operating throughout Britain.
There is evidence to suggest much smaller social groups working
in Wales and the south-west, compared with southern Britain. By the
first century BC a pattern was beginning to emerge, particularly in the
south-east, of a hierarchy dominated by powerful leaders, kings, who
were surrounded by strong and aristocratic noblemen. Caesar tells us
that these were of two classes, 'that of the Druids, the other that of the
Knights. The Druids are concerned with the worship of the gods . . .
they have the right to decide nearly all public and private disputes and
they also pass judgement. The Knights take part in war wherever
there is need and war is declared. It used to happen nearly every year
that they either attacked another tribe or warded off the attacks of
another tribe.' The great majority of Britons belonged to the peasant
classes and were probably little more than slaves. It is likely that they
performed tasks for the aristocracy in return for protection.

It is clear from the large number of hillforts that they could not all
have been the headquarters of kings. Many that were permanently
lived in must have been the bases for knights, with provision for their
vassals. Others may have been supply bases for the tribe. The more
important the individual in control, the grander the hillfort.
Suggestions have been made that in some areas forts were the
products of a group of specialist 'architects' and attention has been
drawn to similarities between the entrances at one fort and those at
another, such as St Catherine's Hill and Danebury (Hampshire).
On other sites irregularities in design and apparent mistakes suggest
that the work was that of beginners experimenting with a design for
the first time, as at Ivinghoe (Buckinghamshire) for example.

We have already made suggestions as to who built the forts. Late
bronze-age farmers set up defences around their settlements and
began the process. Did Celtic immigrants arrive, bring their language
and knowledge of ironworking? It is difficult to explain language as a
result of trade, though metalworking and pottery making can be
learnt by copying and casual contact.

Finally, why were forts built? We have shown that each was defen-
sive in its own way, whether as a walled town, centralised distribution
centre, military barracks or protected farmstead. Can we see a dual
role? Did they serve all the above functions, but at the same time did

the fortification offer a refuge to which the local people could retire in times of conflict? Caesar tells us how the Celts attacked a fort in Gaul: 'They surround the whole circuit of the walls with a large number of men and shower it with stones from all sides, so that the defences are denuded of men. Then they form *testudo,* set fire to the gates and undermine the walls.' According to Celtic literature battles tended to be fought between champions or with chariots in open countryside. Perhaps it was to the fort that combatants retired when all else was lost?

In the future we must try to see the hillfort in its wider surroundings, its natural territory. Work now being carried out is helping to establish what the environment of the fort was like: its satellite farms and villages, its fields and woodlands, its boundaries, industries and cemeteries. Only when we have this total picture can we begin to understand the role played by the fort.

# 7
# Two typical hillforts

Many hillforts have now been partially excavated, some of them large and famous, others small and insignificant. In this book there is room only to consider two average hillforts in more detail. Neither has been fully published and the ideas that I have expressed about them are not necessarily those of the excavators.

### Burrough Hill, Leicestershire (fig. 17)

This trapezoidal fort of 12 acres (4.8 ha) dominates a flat promontory, with wide views north-westwards towards Thorpe. Although it has been dug into on a number of occasions information about it is relatively sparse and relies largely on field observation. The rampart stands highest on the east, where the fort is most vulnerable, adjoining the flat plateau land of the main hillmass. Quarry scoops outside this wall of the fort seem to have provided the drystone which faces the rampart and must have originally stood at least 12 feet (4 m) high. On the steep hillslopes to the north, south and west a scarped ditch was cut, with a counterscarp bank. Some of the quarried stone was taken uphill to build the rampart wall, but the greater amount probably came from internal quarry scoops now obliterated by later ploughing. At the south-east and south-west corners sunken trackways lead up to the fort but are not necessarily original. The hilltop was used as a fairground in medieval times and must have seen much traffic.

The most prominent feature of the fort is the massive inturned entrance 147 feet (45 m) long, which was partially excavated by S.E. Thomas and the writer in 1960. It seems likely that this entrance was redesigned at least three times. At first it took the form of a simple straight-through gap entrance. Later a higher inturn was added 82 feet (25 m) long. Eventually rectangular stone guard chambers were built on to this, the one excavated providing a room 28 feet (8.5 m) by 18 feet (5.5 m). The guard chambers seem to have had lean-to roofs of timber but were probably open to the entrance passage. Hearths were found on the chamber floor. Beyond the guard chamber were double gates leading into the fort. There was insufficient time to find traces of other gates in the long passage, but it is fairly certain that they existed. The road surface in the entrance passage had been renewed three times at its inner end.

A magnetometer survey indicated a small number of storage pits inside the fort and other anomalies that may have been huts. Only storage pits were excavated in 1960 and contained refuse as well as clean soil suggestive of deliberate filling. Surface features indicating huts have long since been destroyed by the medieval ridge and furrow ploughing which is evident both inside and outside the fort.

It seems likely that a fort as large as Burrough Hill was the tribal capital of the Coritani, who occupied this area in the years immediately before the Claudian invasion. The ramparts of the fort are much damaged with many gaps, and this might be interpreted as slighting by the Romans 'on all sides'. Because of the lack of internal excavation, we do not yet know if the fort was filled with buildings as would seem most likely. A tribal capital would warrant administrative and religious buildings, as well as houses and market facilities, particularly since there are no other forts in the neighbourhood. Burrough Hill is a site where further work is very necessary.

### Conderton Camp (Danes Camp), Hereford and Worcester (fig. 18)

Conderton Camp lies on the southern edge of Bredon Hill, an oval-shaped limestone outlier of the Cotswolds covering about 4 square miles (10 sq km). On the north-western side of the hill is the 11 acre (4.5 ha) fort of Bredon Hill, excavated by Thalassa Hencken between 1935 and 1937. Conderton, on a southern spur, is a lop-sided oval in plan and encloses only 3 acres (1.2 ha). Excavation by Nicholas Thomas and the present writer in 1958-9 indicated that the fort was of two periods and occupied by the same people as the larger fort.

There are steep hillslopes on the west, south and east of the fort, but on the north a gentler slope continues up to the summit of Bredon. This gentle slope creates a severe military hazard since the fort is totally overlooked from the north. At the southern tip of the hill is a series of springs which provided a continuous water supply.

At first the fort was roughly oval in shape and the long sides were defended by a bank of rubble and soil piled up behind an irregular stack of limestone blocks about 4 feet (1.2 m) high. Side ditches were never less than 2 to 3 feet (0.6 to 0.9m) deep, with low counterscarp banks. Only along the weak northern side was the rock-cut ditch V-shaped and 7 feet (2 m) deep. The northern bank was about 5 feet (1.5 m) high and its ends, beside the gate, were faced with neatly laid drystone walling. The entrance was at first 28 feet (8.5 m) wide but was reduced to less than half that width by a wooden stockade that was erected soon after its initial construction. The excavations failed to find the southern entrance, which may never have been more than a gap without a gateway, though the ditch ends at that point were deeper. In this first phase, datable perhaps to around 300 BC, the fort was little more than a cattle enclosure, perhaps serving the larger fort $1\frac{1}{4}$ miles (2 km) to the north-west. If there were any huts inside the enclosure, they have not been identified.

At a later period the enclosure was reduced in size. Drystone, perhaps from the dismantled southern part of the rampart, was built into a thick wall that cut across the middle of the fort and isolated about 2 acres (0.8 ha). The new wall was monumental in style, well built of layers of stone, with an inturned gateway at its centre (fig. 19). A passage 23 feet (7 m) long and 20 feet (6 m) wide led to a narrow gateway only 7 feet (2.1 m) wide. The road surface at this point was well worn. A circular hut just inside the gate was probably a guard hut. Perhaps at about the same time as the fort was reduced in size, the northern entrance was remodelled with long inturns. This was later completely closed by building a thick drystone wall right across it.

Inside the 2 acre (0.8 ha) fort were about a dozen circular huts. Parts of six were identified and shown to have been about 20 feet (6 m) in diameter, with wall bases of drystone and the roofs probably thatched. Entrances faced the north-west. About sixty storage pits had been dug inside the enclosure, with diameters and depths of 4 to 7 feet (1.2 to 2.0 m) (fig. 20). Clearly they were not all contemporary and from the way in which they cut into each other it was obvious that the positions of earlier ones had been forgotten when new ones were dug. Some of the pits were lined with drystone walling, others with basketwork and perhaps clay. Most had been used for rubbish after they had been abandoned for grain storage, though one was almost certainly a latrine pit. In the south-east of the camp a quarry scoop seems to have been used as a working place.

Pottery from Conderton was of Cunliffe's Croft Ambrey-Bredon style with 'duck' motifs and incised lines, manufactured in the Malvern area some 15 miles (25 km) away, and comparable with the material from the 11 acre (4.5 ha) fort of Bredon Hill. Although there was no evidence of a violent end to the fort, there are suggestions that it was deserted very hastily, with the remains of mutton stews left lying on the hut floors, not even to be eaten by scavenging dogs. Perhaps the inhabitants retreated to the big Bredon Hill fort, where some of them may eventually have met a violent end.

We are probably right in seeing Conderton first as a cattle enclosure, subservient to Bredon Hill fort. Later it developed independently as a small outlying village, concerned with activities on the south-east side of the hill. The vulnerability of the northern entrance was always troublesome and the inhabitants first of all reduced it with timber and later blocked it with a stone wall. Eventually they deserted Conderton in favour of the main fortress to the north-west.

# 8
# Some hillforts to visit

*Hillfort. National Grid Reference.*
Almondbury, West Yorkshire. SE 152140
Beacon Hill, Hampshire. SU 458572
Bigbury, Kent. TR 117575
Blackbury Castle, Devon. SY 187924
Bosherston, Pembroke, Dyfed. SR 971948
Burrough Hill, Leicestershire. SK 761119
Bredon Hill, Hereford and Worcester. SO 958400
Bury Hill, Hampshire. SU 346435
The Caburn, East Sussex. TQ 444089
Caer Caradoc, Church Stretton, Shropshire. SO 477953
Caer Caradoc, Clun, Shropshire. SO 310758
Caer y Twr, Anglesey, Gwynedd. SH 219829
Caesar's Camp, Wimbledon, London. TQ 224711
Carlwark, Derbyshire. SK 260815
Carn Brea, Cornwall. SW 686407
Carn Fadrun, Caernarvon, Gwynedd. SH 280352
Castell Odo, Caernarvon, Gwynedd. SH 187284
Castle Dore, Cornwall. SX 103548
Chalbury, Dorset. SY 695838
Chanctonbury Ring, West Sussex. TQ 139120
Chun Castle, Cornwall. SW 405339
Cissbury, West Sussex. TQ 139080
Clare, Suffolk. TL 769459
Conway Mountain, Caernarvon, Gwynedd. SH 760778
Credenhill, Hereford and Worcester. SO 450445
Croft Ambrey, Hereford and Worcester. SO 445668
Danebury, Hampshire. SU 323376
Dinas Dinlle, Caernarvon, Gwynedd. SH 437563
Dinas Emrys, Caernarvon, Gwynedd. SH 606492
Dinorwig, Caernarvon, Gwynedd. SH 550653
Ffridd Faldwyn, Montgomery, Powys. SO 217969
Figsbury Rings, Wiltshire. SU 188338
Foel Fenlli, Denbigh, Clwyd, SJ 163601
Garn Boduan, Caernarvon, Gwynedd. SH 310393
Gurnard's Head, Cornwall. SW 433387

Hambledon Hill, Dorset. ST 845126
Hembury Castle, Devon. ST 112031
Hengistbury Head, Dorset. SZ 170908
Hod Hill, Dorset. ST 857106
Hollingbury, East Sussex. TQ 322078
Honington, Lincolnshire. SK 954423
Hunsbury, Northamptonshire. SP 738583
Ingleborough, North Yorkshire. SD 741747
Ivinghoe Beacon, Buckinghamshire. SP 960169
Ladle Hill, Hampshire. SU 749568
Llanmelin, Gwent. ST 460925
Llanymynech Hill, Montgomery, Powys. SJ 265220
Lordenshaws, Northumberland. NZ 054993
Lydney, Gloucestershire. SO 616027
Maen Castle, Cornwall. SW 347257
Maiden Castle, Cheshire. SJ 498528
Maiden Castle, Dorset. SY 669885
Mam Tor, Derbyshire. SK 128838
Membury, Devon. ST 282028
Milber Down, Devon. SX 884698
Moel Trigarn, Pembroke, Dyfed. SN 158336
Oldbury, Kent. TQ 582566
Old Oswestry, Shropshire. SJ 296310
Old Sarum, Wiltshire. SU 137327
Old Winchester Hill, Hampshire. SU 641206
Pen Dinas, Cardigan, Dyfed. SN 584804
Pen-y-Gaer, Caernarvon, Gwynedd. SH 750693
Quarley Hill, Hampshire. SU 262423
Rainsborough, Northamptonshire. SP 526348
The Ringses, Northumberland. NU 014327
St Catherine's Hill, Hampshire. SU 484276
St David's Head, Pembroke, Dyfed. SM 722279
Skelmore Heads, Lancashire. SD 274751
South Cadbury, Somerset. ST 628252
Stanwick, North Yorkshire. NZ 180115
Staple Howe, North Yorkshire. SE 898749
Tregeare Rounds, Cornwall. SX 033800
Tre'r Ceiri, Caernarvon, Gwynedd. SH 373446
The Trundle, West Sussex. SU 877110
Wandlebury, Cambridgeshire. TL 493534
Warham, Norfolk. TF 944409
Winklebury, Wiltshire. ST 952217
Worlebury, Avon. ST 314625
The Wrekin, Shropshire. SJ 629082
Yarnbury, Wiltshire. SU 035403
Yeavering Bell, Northumberland. NT 928293

# 9
# Select bibliography

Alcock, L. *'By South Cadbury is that Camelot . . . .'* 1972.
Bradley, R. and Ellison, A. *Rams Hill.* 1975.
Cunliffe, B. *Danebury. Anatomy of an Iron Age Hillfort.* 1983.
Cunliffe, B. *Iron Age Communities in Britain.* 1978.
Forde-Johnston, J. *Hillforts of the Iron Age in England and Wales.* 1976.
Guilbert G. (editor). *Hill-Fort Studies.* 1981.
Harding, D. W. (editor). *Hillforts: Later Prehistoric Earthworks in Britain and Ireland.* 1976.
Harding, D. W. *Celts in Conflict: Hillfort Studies 1927-77.* 1979.
Hogg, A. H. A. *Hill-Forts of Britain.* 1975.
Hogg, A. H. A. *British Hill-Forts: An Index.* 1979.
Jesson, M. and Hill, D. *The Iron Age and its Hill-Forts.* 1971.
Jewell, P. A. (editor). *The Experimental Earthwork on Overton Down, Wiltshire, 1960.* 1963.
Ordnance Survey. *Southern Britain in the Iron Age.* 1962.
Wheeler, R. E. M. *Maiden Castle, Dorset.* 1943.

**Guidebooks to hillforts worth visiting**
Dyer, J. *Southern England: An Archaeological Guide.* 1973.
Dyer, J. *Penguin Guide to Prehistoric England and Wales.* 1981.
Hogg, A. H. A. *Hill-Forts of Britain.* 1975.
Houlder, C. *Wales: An Archaeological Guide.* 1974.
Thomas, N. *Guide to Prehistoric England.* 1976.
Wainwright, R. *A Guide to Prehistoric Remains in Britain.* 1978.

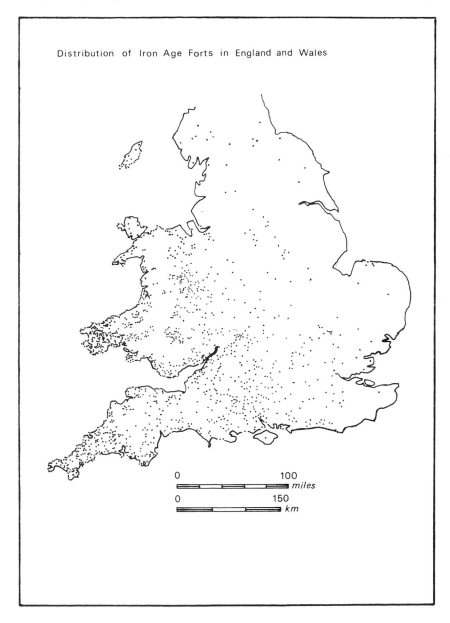

Distribution of Iron Age Forts in England and Wales

**Fig. 1.** Distribution of iron-age forts in England and Wales.

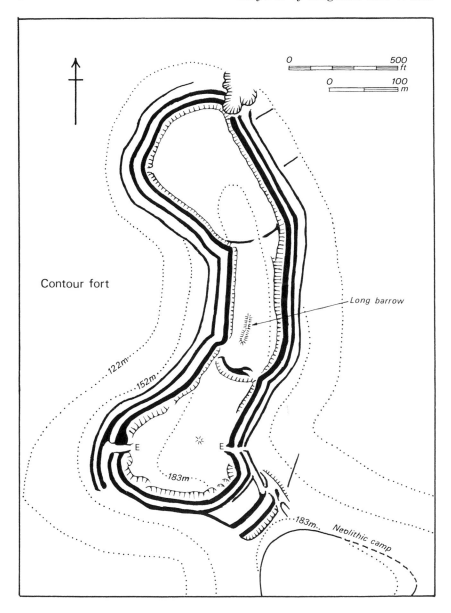

**Fig. 2.** A typical contour fort: Hambledon Hill (Dorset). In all plans the thick line represents the rampart.

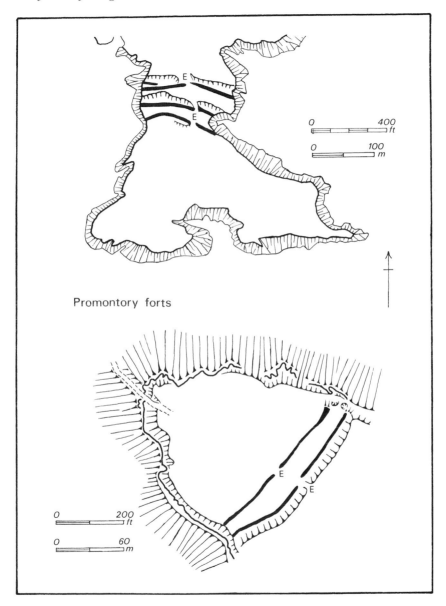

Promontory forts

**Fig. 3.** *(Above)* The Rumps (Cornwall), an example of a cliff-castle. *(Below)* Combs Moss (Derbyshire), a typical promontory fort.

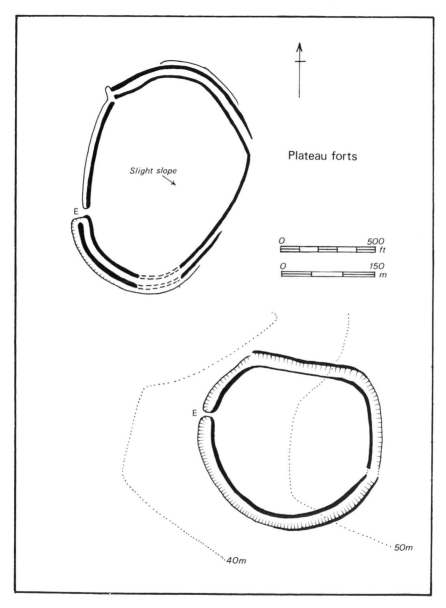

Plateau forts

Slight slope

E

0 ——————— 500
                    ft
0 ——————— 150
                    m

E

40m

50m

**Fig. 4.** Plateau forts. *(Above)* The Aubreys (Hertfordshire). *(Below)* Caesar's Camp (Greater London).

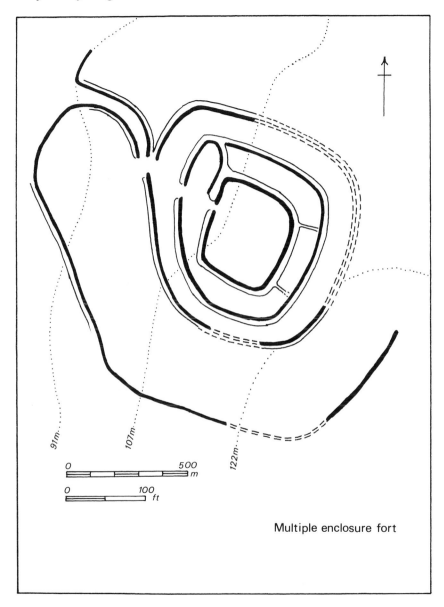

**Fig. 5.** Multiple-enclosure or hillslope fort: Milber Down Camp (Devon).

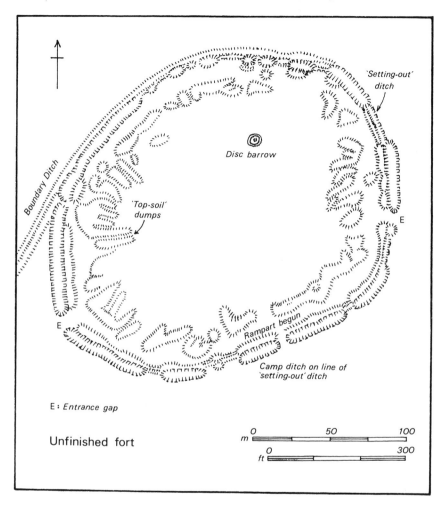

Disc barrow

'Setting-out' ditch

Boundary Ditch

'Top-soil' dumps

E

Rampart begun

Camp ditch on line of 'setting-out' ditch

E

E : *Entrance gap*

Unfinished fort

m  0        50       100

ft  0              300

**Fig. 6.** Ladle Hill unfinished hillfort, Hampshire (after S. Piggott).

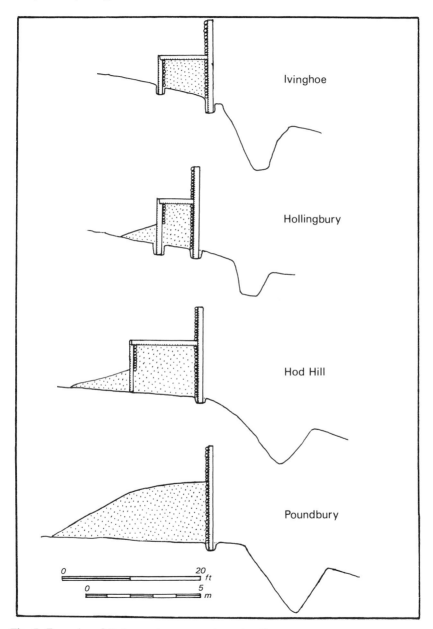

**Fig. 7.** Examples of timber or box rampart construction.

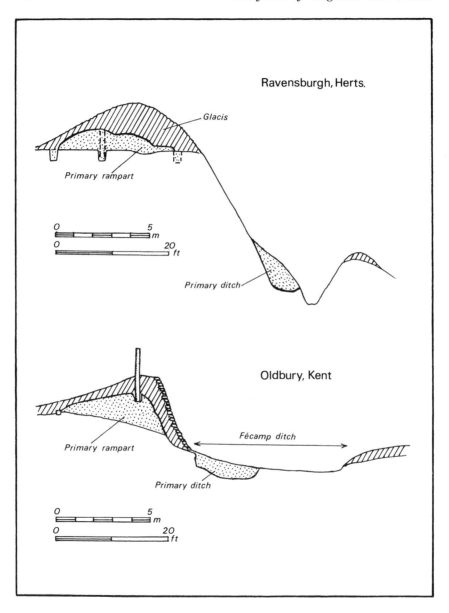

**Fig. 8.** Glacis and Fécamp style ramparts.

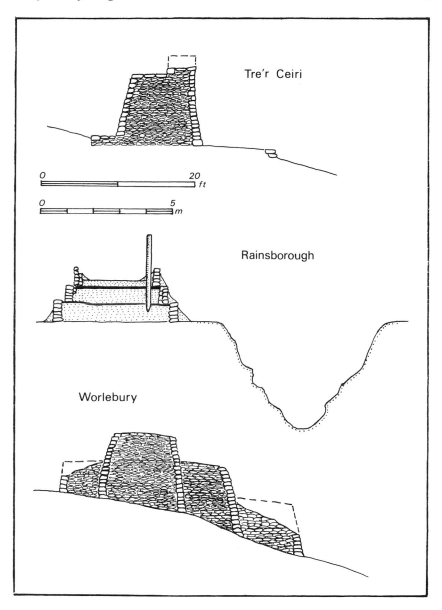

**Fig. 9.** Stone-faced ramparts.

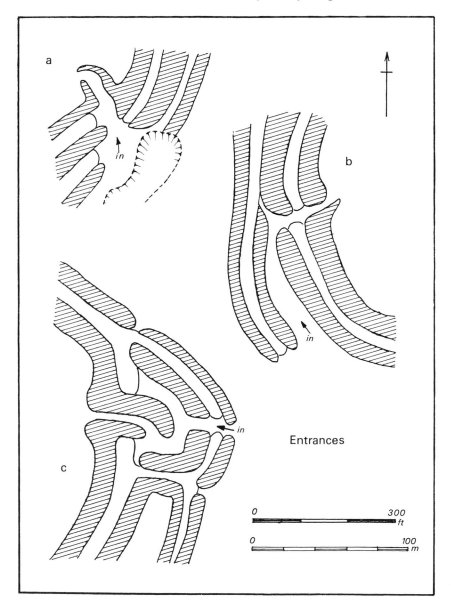

**Fig. 10.** Entrance types: (a) inturned (Painswick Beacon, Gloucestershire); (b) staggered (Hambledon south-west, Dorset); (c) elaborate (Danebury, Hampshire).

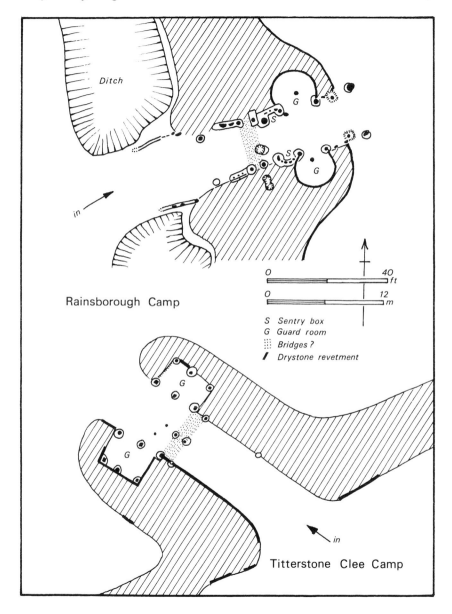

**Fig. 11.** Hillfort entrances with guard chambers (after M. Avery and B. O'Neil).

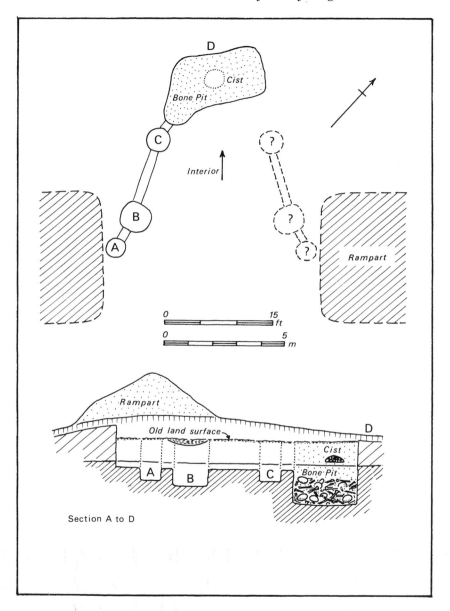

**Fig. 12.** South-eastern entrance of Maiden Bower, Bedfordshire, with central pit containing human bones.

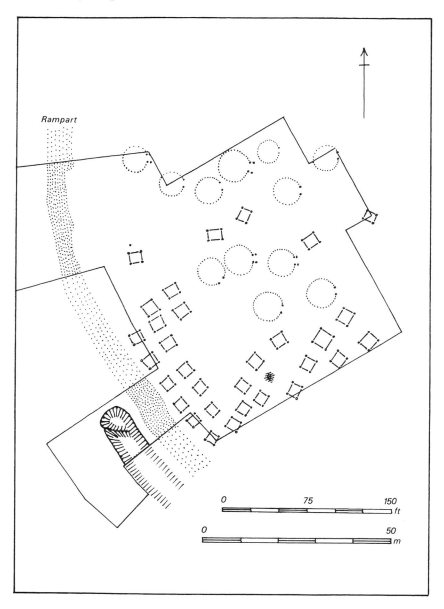

**Fig. 13.** Moel y Gaer, Rhosesmor (Clwyd). Four-poster and stake-walled circular houses of Phase 2 (after Graeme Guilbert).

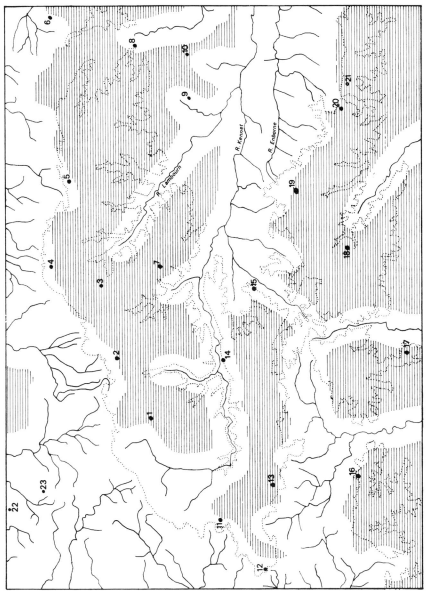

**Fig. 14.** The distribution of north Wessex hillforts and their relation to land more than a mile from a permanent water supply (shaded). The forts are not all contemporary (after B. Cunliffe, with additions). North is to the left.

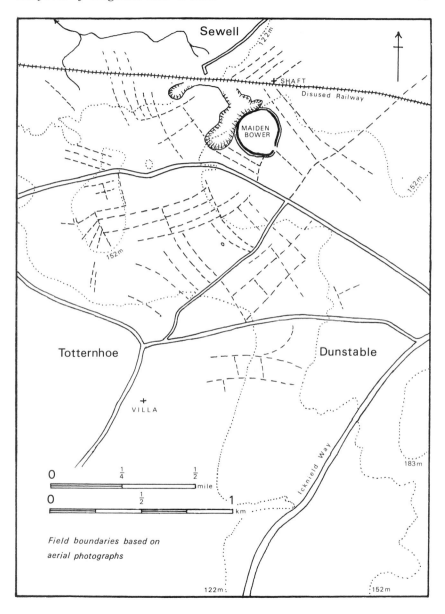

**Fig. 15.** The prehistoric field system around Maiden Bower plateau fort (Bedfordshire).

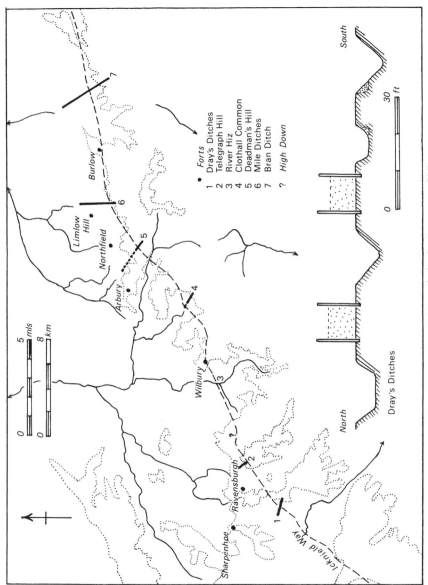

**Fig. 16.** Iron-age territorial boundaries in the eastern Chilterns.

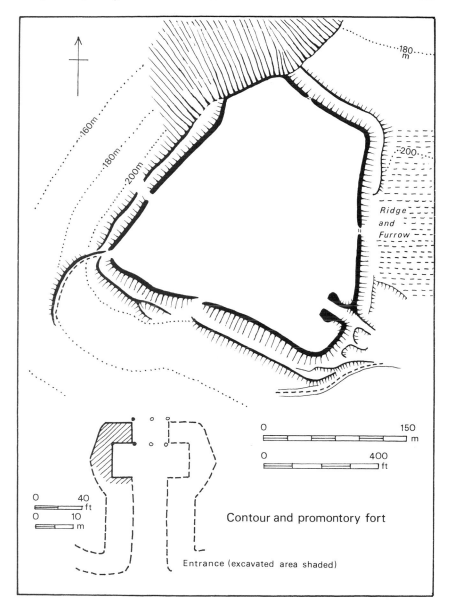

**Fig. 17.** Burrough Hill (Leicestershire) is both a promontory and a contour fort. Inset is the inturned entrance showing the area excavated in 1960 (after S. E. Thomas).

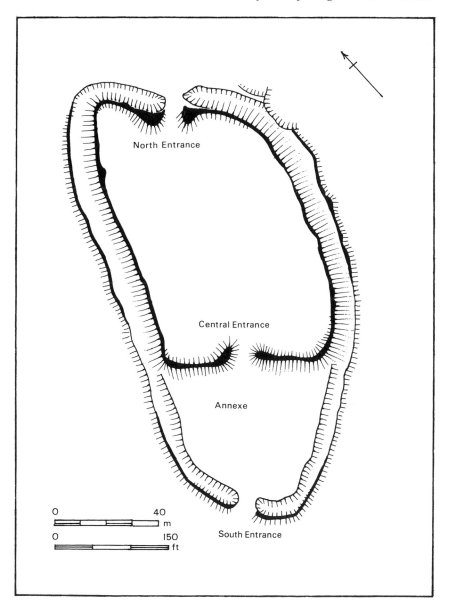

**Fig. 18.** Conderton Camp (Hereford and Worcester). The ditch surrounding the annexe belongs to Phase 1. The remainder formed the fort in Phase 2 (after Nicholas Thomas).

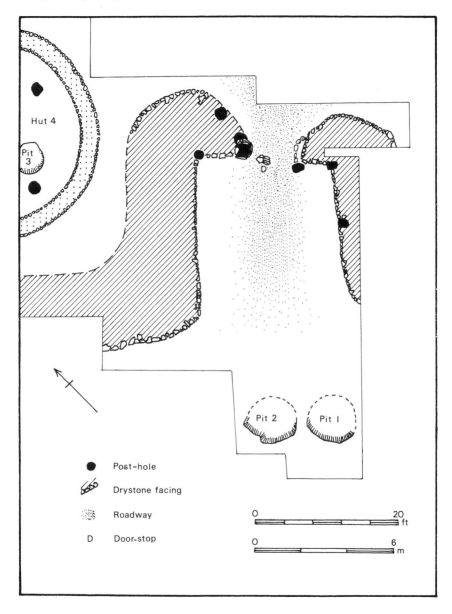

**Fig. 19.** The central entrance of Conderton Camp, constructed in Phase 2. Hut 4 was probably a guard hut (after Nicholas Thomas).

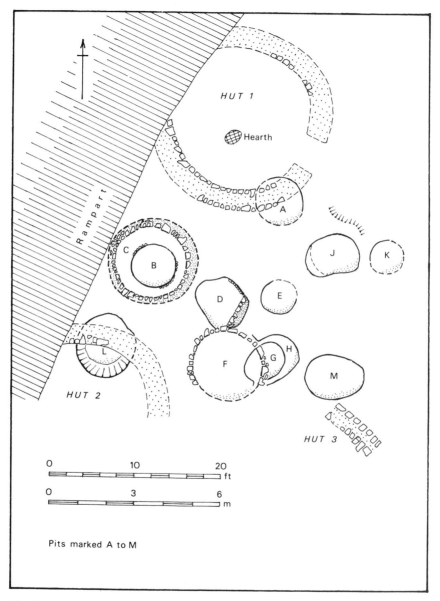

**Fig. 20.** Part of the storage pit complex at Conderton Camp. Notice how some of the pits have cut into earlier ones at least three times (F, G. H) and how huts 1 and 2 are later than pits A and L (after Nicholas Thomas).

**Plate 1.** The contour fort of Uffington Castle (Oxfordshire), from the south-east, with the Ridgeway in the foreground. (J. K. St Joseph: Crown copyright.)

**Plate 2.** The bivallate fort of Sodbury (Gloucestershire), with a steep drop on the furthest side. The ditch in the foreground appears to be unfinished. (Aerofilms Ltd.)

**Plate 3.** The multiple-enclosure fort of Clovelly Dykes, Devon. (J. K. St Joseph: Crown copyright.)

**Plate 4.** One of the highest hillforts in England, Ingleborough in North Yorkshire. The stone rampart is badly damaged. Notice the hut circles inside the fort. (J. K. St Joseph: Crown copyright.)

**Plate 5.** The great contour fort of the British Camp (or Herefordshire Beacon). The highest point is crowned by a Norman castle motte. (J. K. St Joseph: Crown copyright.)

**Plate 6.** The univallate fort of The Trundle at Goodwood (West Sussex) occupies the same site as a neolithic causewayed camp, just visible at the centre of the earthworks. (J. K. St Joseph: Crown copyright.)

**Plate 7.** The unfinished hillfort of Ladle Hill (Hampshire) with the piles of spoil from the ditches still visible inside the ditch. Notice the disc-barrow on the right. (J. K. St Joseph: Crown copyright.)

**Plate 8.** The north-east side of Uleybury promontory fort (Gloucestershire). The terrace on the left has probably been formed by digging out material to build the bank.

**Plate 9.** Postholes of the early rampart of Moel y Gaer, Rhosesmor (Clwyd). Drystone walling stood between the posts. (G. Guilbert.)

**Plate 10.** Tre'r Ceiri (Gwynedd): some of the circular huts in this very exposed fort were occupied in the first and second centuries AD. (S. W. Feather.)

**Plate 11.** Burrough Hill (Leicestershire). Notice the long inturned entrance on the left. The ground drops steeply on the right-hand side. (J. K. St Joseph: Crown copyright.)

**Plate 12.** A storage pit at Burrough Hill, containing an iron-age pot and two quern stones.

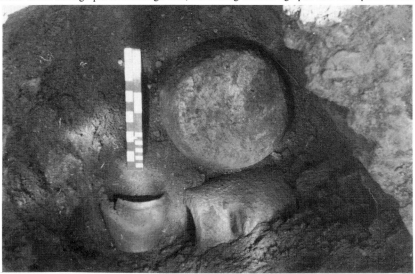

**Plate 13.** The excavated south-west gate of Cadbury Castle hillfort (Somerset). On the right side of the passage is a guard chamber cut into the rock of the hillside. (Camelot Research Committee.)

**Plate 14.** The complex entrance to Danebury (Hampshire).

**Plate 15.** Looking south-west across Conderton Camp (Hereford and Worcester). The central and northern entrances can be clearly seen. (J. E. Hancock.)

**Plate 16.** One of the huts at Conderton Camp. It was approximately 20 feet (6 m) in diameter. The entrance is in the foreground. Part of the wall has been rebuilt on the left. (Nicholas Thomas.)

**Plate 17.** The restricted entrance of Chun Castle (Cornwall). The entrance is staggered and it is approached from the right-hand side of the picture.

**Plate 18.** The irregular line of postholes of the Dray's Ditches iron-age boundary dyke (Bedfordshire). It was constructed as a box rampart and resembles the work at Ivinghoe Beacon 10 miles (16 km) to the west.

# Index